Run an Election Campaign

Project Management Style

By

Pádraig Boyle

Boyle Practical Project Management

© 2020 BPPM

www.bppm.ie

1 Run an Election Campaign

This document outlines the Project Planning elements necessary to "Run for Election" that will give candidates a roadmap to follow to get elected as a member of parliament in whichever. jurisdiction for which you are seeking to represent. It serves as a reference for local and national election teams. Canvassers can read through the entire plan so that they have some understanding of the whole process and the success framework in detail.

The campaign plan is the foundation to build the campaign upon. A campaign plan created with the help of your advisors, and past candidates gives you the roadmap for the run up until the day of the election and the following week.Some things considered here include:

☐**Political Environment**: What is the priority issue your voters have? What are your opponents' issues and policies?

☐**Targeting and Demographics**: –The areas you would focus on based on the makeup of the voters living there. How can you target them?

☐**Campaign Message and Issues**:   – Outline   the core message of your campaign. How does it relate to the issues you focus on?

☐**Communication Plan**: – The   campaign   message distribution methods. How do you plan to get press coverage?

☐**Area Outreach Plan**:   – How do you plan your door to door pamphlet distribution using volunteers?

□**Campaign Budget**: – What would be the budget and estimated cost for every task?

□**Funding Plan:** – What methods will you use to fund the campaign?

□**Campaign Timeline:** – How will you meet the deadlines for each milestone and activity?

□**Staffing:** – Who do you have to fill the key roles like Campaign Manager and Office Manager?

1.1 Initiation

A political campaign can be an exciting experience. A great deal will happen between the beginning of a campaign and a week after election day and with a little forethought and planning, you can be prepared for all the twists and turns and, in many cases, control the situation.

This plan is designed to help you anticipate what will happen and be better prepared. While the given political landscape is an important factor in any campaign, in many cases the most important factor - the difference between winning and losing - is what goes on inside the campaign.

Are You Ready to Run for Election? It is critical to make sure that you have thought everything through before announcing that you are running for political office. Here are some considerations:

• understand the time commitment

• fulfill the eligibility criteria to run for election in your area

• be confident that you can balance family life, work life with running an election campaign

• have funds for your campaign

<u>Why Political Campaigns Fail</u>

There are four types of election campaigns that have little or no chance to achieve victory:

The first is the campaign that has no persuasive or unique message to deliver to voters.

The second is the campaign does not have a clear idea of which voters it wants to persuade.

The third is the campaign that has a unique, persuasive message and a clear idea of which voters it wants to persuade but has no practical plan of what to do between the beginning of the campaign and the day of the election, to persuade these voters.

Lastly, the fourth type of campaign is one that has a clear message, a clear idea of its voters and a plan to get to Election Day but it fails to follow through on or execute the plan.

1.1.1   The "As Is" Analysis

On an operational basis record how long, you have been operating in the community and the issues you have taken positions on:

(a)

(b)

(c)

Record the actions that you have already taken, in addressing these issues:

(a)

(b)

(c)

Record the successful outcomes you have had to date:

(a)

(b)

(c)

The social issues affecting our community currently are:

(a)

(b)

(c)

The record of the "as is" is an iterative process that you can update as you proceed with further research.

1.1.2   The "To Be" Analysis

Considering the reasons for failed campaigns the political campaign planned here will be one that takes the time to target voters, develops a persuasive message and follows through on a reasonable and practical plan to engage with and persuade those voters.

This written campaign plan defines the overall political landscape, the strategy and resources required to get to the day of the election. While it is true that every campaign is unique, there are some basic principles that can be applied to any election campaign. This plan is designed to help you apply these basic principles to your unique campaign.

This campaign will communicate a persuasive message to people who will vote. The actual planning process is designed to take the campaign through a step-by-step process to develop a written campaign plan.

This plan cannot give you all the answers to all the problems your campaign will face. It cannot tell you what your campaign message should be. It cannot tell you who your most likely supporters are. It cannot tell you what the most effective methods of contacting voters in your region are. What it can do is provide the questions that will help you think through the planning process in a thorough and methodical way. BPPM's methodology can help you customise your individual campaign. Too often, politicians "in situ" believe that they hold the winning strategy "in their heads." They have no strategy at all and are wandering aimlessly. Too often the candidate and the campaign manager believe that they are following a single strategy, only to find out later that their opinions about the strategy are completely at odds. A written campaign plan agreed upon by the candidate, the campaign manager and all the key advisors, would help avoid such problems. The rule is simple - if a plan is not written down, the plan does not exist.

Once you have the written plan, you must follow that plan in a disciplined way. As with any plan, it is only as good as its implementation. All campaigns must be flexible to changing circumstances, but these changes should be carefully considered and weighed against the original research and strategy laid out in the plan.

A political campaign is an intense experience and, when done correctly, it is also a lot of hard work. There are no tricks or short cuts to winning the confidence of the voters. A political campaign can also be an exhilarating, rewarding and fun experience.

A poorly planned campaign is often distracted by the day's events, by things the opponent's campaign does or by things the press says, spending more time reacting to outside factors than promoting its own agenda.

Every campaign is different and unique. While certain basic principles can be applied to each campaign, it is important to have a complete understanding of the situation and the conditions in which your campaign will be waged. At some point in almost every campaign, someone says, "it is different here" or "you are not considering our particular situation". Research is where you start and where you consider the differences and peculiarities of each campaign. It is here that you have the chance to demonstrate just how different your situation really is.

1.1.3   Charter

Goal: Setting a strategic campaign goal of achieving the votes that are needed to win is the key to success. The ultimate purpose of this political campaign is to serve the people by getting elected.

Stakeholders: The primary stakeholders are the candidate, the candidate's family, and the campaign team. The secondary project stakeholders are the constituents, advertisers, the media, and other candidates.

Budget & Funding: The budget for the project is €-- and is funded from personal savings and donations. This is exclusive of the costs of volunteers in terms of time.

Timescale: The election will be held on Day, Date, Month, Year.

Project Team Resources: The Project Team Resources required are the candidate and the campaign team inclusive of volunteers.

Signed

_____   Date: _____

Project Sponsor

1.1.4   Success Framework

The basis for succeeding with this project is through satisfying the success criteria. The critical success factors are represented in the middle of the **Theoretical Success Framework Diagram**, representing their relationship to achieving both project and product objectives and their influence on satisfying the success criteria. The objectives, the success factors and the success criteria are agreed by the primary stakeholders following a series of brainstorming sessions and a consultation process.

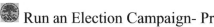
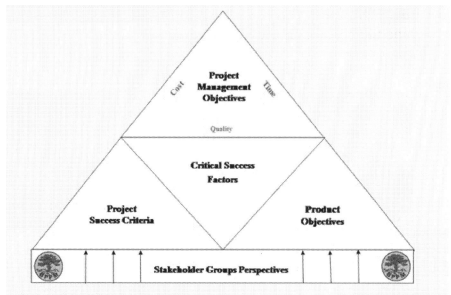

Boyle Practical Project Management Success Framework

1.1.4.1   Project Team Resources

After making the decision to run for election the selection of resources is the first order of business for the election campaign. The positions that need to be assigned are campaign manager for oversight of all the operations, a person to answer the phones and deal with general office, and volunteers to help with canvassing. Other roles such as press secretary, media content writer and others are dependent on the size of the campaign and type of election.

1.1.4.1.1 The Role of the Candidate

The most important person in any political campaign is the candidate and the candidate's time is the most precious resource that the campaign has. If the candidate or the campaign wastes that time, it can never be replaced. It is therefore important to understand the role of the candidate and the best use of their time.

That role is to meet and persuade people to vote for you as the candidate. Once the strategy has been decided, you the candidate need to leave the running of the campaign to the campaign manager and others and concentrate entirely on meeting and persuading as many voters as possible.

1.1.4.1.2 Select Campaign Manager

Select someone for the role of the campaign manager in which you as the candidate have complete confidence to run the campaign. Too often candidates want to run their own campaign. They either do not choose a campaign manager or choose someone they think they can manipulate. In either case they end up spending too much time making decisions that should be left to someone else, which takes time from their main job, meeting voters and spreading their message.

A campaign manager makes sure the candidate is scheduled to meet voters and gives leadership to those who will deal with the press, the money, the other methods of voter contact and everything else planned during the campaign. The campaign manager is responsible for keeping the campaign project schedule up to date and distributing it to everyone in the campaign who needs to keep abreast of the activities.

1.1.4.1.3 Select Campaign Team

The more times an individual has been involved in past political campaigns, the better prepared they should be for the next political campaign. Politics has become specialised and therefore having the advice, assistance, or benefit of someone who has experienced the various phases of a campaign can be extremely helpful to a candidate and a campaign. If you know people with campaign experience, try to get them on board.

•Finance Chair:

This can be a spouse, relative or close friend. Ideally this person has some experience with finances and is confident in their ability to balance the books as candidates must maintain proper records of all transactions relating to spending on their election campaign and retain receipts, invoices or vouchers for inspection by the relevant authority, if required.

Press Secretary/Communications / Social Media:

This role or roles will help you create press releases, emails, spell check everything you write, assists with any speeches, and help manage your social media. Look for someone in your network with communications, marketing, or public relations experience.

Volunteers:

These are the people who want to be a part of your team and help in any way that they can. These people will help make calls, knock on doors, attend events, and countless other tasks. Close friends, young people, 3rd level students and retired people are often great fits for this role. Volunteers need to be trained to stick to the campaign message and to the agreed process and not be side-tracked.

1.1.4.2 Project Outputs

The product objectives and the project management objectives are:

Engage with Groups	Become the "Go To" Person
Identify Specific Local Public Needs	Evaluate Current Infrastructure
Exemplify a Safe and Healthy Lifestyle	Encourage Protection of Human Rights
Advocate for Compliance with Laws	Operate within Budget

1.1.4.3 Critical Success Factors

The Critical Success Factors for this Election Campaign are:

Realistic Campaign Plan	Practical Objectives
Accomplished Campaign Team	Process for Engagement
Clear Campaign Message	

1.1.4.4 Success Criteria

The criteria as drawn up by the stakeholders are in the table below. The units of measurement after the election to determine the success rate against the targets. Getting elected is not sufficient to satisfy the specifications as set out as criteria for success.

11

All your voter contact activities should be quantifiable. You voter contact goals should not include "establishing good media relations" because such a goal does not mean anything in real terms. How many events will you hold? How many press releases will you send out?

Campaign Outputs	Success Criteria Measurement Units	Target
Engage with Groups	No of Groups spoken to and met with for more than a 30-minute meeting	10
Identify Specific Local Public Needs	How many needs noted and followed up on	50
Evaluate Current Infrastructure	How many practical solutions offered based on evaluations carried out	5
Exemplify a Safe and Healthy Lifestyle	Leading by example. Real identifiable measures taken during the campaign.	3
Encourage Protection of Human Rights	No. of issues Included in messages	5
Advocate for Compliance with Bye Laws	How many issues raised and followed up	3

The risks, their likely impact and the necessary response are set out in the following table:

1.1.4.5 Risks

No.	Risk Identified	Likely Impact	Risk Response
1	Missing Required Quota	Financial Hardship.	Spend only what you can afford to lose.
2	Candidate or Campaign Manager Gets Sick or Injured During Campaign.	Loss of Resource time. Activities Left Undone.	A robust contingency plan identifies and considers risks in advance and develops a plan of action which can be effectively communicated when required. Identify stand-ins.
3	Lack of Face-to-Face Conversations	Low Supporter Voter Turnout	Train volunteers to complete high-quality, face-to-face conversations in every household that urge them to vote.

Risk 1:   **The Required Quota**

There are variations in electoral systems, but the most common systems are first-past-the-post voting, proportional representation and ranked voting. With a first past-the-post electoral system, voters cast their vote for a candidate of their choice, and the candidate who receives the most votes wins. Proportional representation is based on divisions in an electorate with the objective of having these divisions reflected proportionately in the elected body which is decided through proportional representation with a single transferable vote. Ranked voting is any election voting system in which voters use a ranked (or preferential) ballot to rank choices in a sequence on the ordinal scale: 1st, 2nd, 3rd. Many countries use a mixed electoral system that combine elements of both non-proportional and proportional systems.

A quota is used in elections held under the single transferable vote system. The quota is the minimum number of votes a candidate must receive to be elected. In an electoral system, a deposit is the sum of money that a candidate for an elected office, is required to pay to an electoral authority before he or she is permitted to stand for election.

In the typical case, the deposit collected is repaid to the candidate after the poll if the candidate obtains a specified proportion of the votes cast. The purpose of the deposit is to reduce the number of candidates with no realistic chance of winning a seat. If the candidate does not achieve the refund threshold, the deposit is forfeited.

In this context you must decide how much of your personal finances you are prepared to risk on the campaign that may or may not be successful

Risk 2 Injured or Sickness during campaign.

To meet staffing crises that may emerge during voting election have a contingency for reserves of key staff and volunteers to be available. These could be friends that you have on standby. Allowance should also be made for allocated staff not reporting for canvassing duty.

Risk 3 Lack of face-to-face conversations

Impersonal methods of campaigning have consistently failed to produce cost-effective results and when

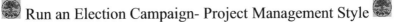

canvassers fail to interact with voters, the impacts they leave are minimal.

Some campaign volunteers often rush through neighbourhoods, hurrying to distribute leaflets and often fail to reach most voters with any real interactions and often do not have any conversations with voters at all.

Research shows that having an actual conversation is crucial to influence voters. Canvassing seems to work best when voters engage in a genuine conversation about why voting is important and that authentic exchanges usually have a favourable impact for the candidate.

It is important that volunteer canvassers have practical training or experience in engaging in a meaningful way with voters on the campaign trail. Making notes of issues that can be examined for potential follow up is crucial. Develop a process for engagement with voters during door to door canvass.

1.1.5 Constraints

The project inputs explain how the product will be done and are defined, by the work breakdown structure, responsibility chart, schedule, and budget. These inputs are further decomposed into work package activities and tasks. These activities are constrained by time, cost, and quality of interaction.

1.1.5.1 Work Breakdown Structure

The activities required to deliver the output objectives are:

PRODUCT BREAKDOWN STRUCTURE						
1.2.1 Election Requirements	**1.2.2** Organise Campaign Team	**1.2.3** Research Candidates	**1.2.4** Examine Demographics	**1.2.5** Target Voters	**1.2.6** Develop Campaign Message	**1.2.7** Implement Voter Contact Plan
1.2.1.1 Comply with Regulations	**1.2.2.1** Define Campaign Structure	**1.2.3.1** Do a SWOT of Yourself	**1.2.4.1** Examine the Electoral Register	**1.2.5.1** Geographic Targeting	**1.2.6.1** Research the Local Issues	**1.2.7.1** Door to Door Canvassing
1.2.1.2 Register Candidacy	**1.2.2.2** Organise Volunteers Roles	**1.2.3.2** Do a SWOT of Opponents	**1.2.4.2** Study Census Data	**1.2.5.2** Demographic Targeting	**1.2.6.2** Message Style	**1.2.7.2** Literature Handouts
	1.2.2.3 Upskill Volunteers		**1.2.4.3** Look at the Geography of the Area	**1.2.5.3** Non Target Groups		**1.2.7.3** Postal Mail
	1.2.2.4 Seek Civic Groups Support			**1.2.5.4** Study Previous Election Statistics		**1.2.7.4** Get Out Your Vote
	1.2.2.5 Political Party					**1.2.7.5** Posters
	1.2.2.6 Determine Volunteer Commitment					**1.2.7.6** Informal Meetings
						1.2.7.7 Printed Press Media
						1.2.7.8 Audio & Visual Media
						1.2.7.9 Website & Social Media
						1.2.7.10 Implement Polling Day Itinerary

These steps include:

1. Doing the research necessary to Comply with Election Requirements.
2. Organise Campaign Team
3. Research Candidates
4. Examine Demographics
5. Target voters
6. Develop a campaign message
7. Contact Voters
8. Implement Polling Day Itinerary

These product work inputs are decomposed into work packages. The WBS below is a picture of the project inputs subdivided into hierarchical units of work and represented as a tree.

1.1.5.2   Time Schedule

1. Elections are date driven. A campaign plan is put together by starting from one week after the election date or an anticipated election date. and working backwards. The ideal scenario is that you are ever ready for an election by connecting with the electorate and dealing with the issues on an ongoing basis.

4. Plan for the resources needed to accomplish each activity. As we look at the schedule timeline, we will determine for each week how many people and how much money will be needed for the activities planned for that week.

5. Plan within the election legislation. Register by a certain date and adhere to dates by which certain activities must be accomplished and dates before or after which other activities are prohibited.

The campaign manager may use the detail within this document to assist with the development of the schedule for your campaign that will include all the dates and all the activities of the campaign.

The campaign manager will add to this schedule any events or meetings that you the candidate must attend and that are not already included. The campaign manager deals with invitations and decides if an event is important enough to attend and ways to decline invitations that the campaign decides are not important.

The schedule distinguishes between activities that will require you the candidate and those that will be handled by the campaign manager and volunteers. Because certain voter contact activities will happen over a long period of time and overlap with other activities, the schedule has a timeline of events that will provide more details about time, money and people involved in each activity. Work package activity durations deduced by the project team may look something like this for a fictitious local area election.

WBS	Activity	Duration
1	Run an Election Campaign	168 days
1.1	Project Initiation	92 days
1.1.1	The "As Is" Analysis	3 days
1.1.2	The "To Be" Analysis	10 days
1.1.3	Project Charter	2 days
1.1.4	Success Framework	53. days
1.1.5	Constraints	24 days
1.2	Product Work Inputs	106 days
1.2.1	Election Requirements	85 days
1.2.2	Organise Campaign Team	12 days
1.2.3	Research Candidates	45 days
1.2.4	Examine Demographics	7 days
1.2.5	Target Voters	10 days
1.2.6	Develop Campaign Message	4 days
1.2.7	Implement Voter Contact Plan	35 days
1.3	Closeout	7 days
1.3.1	The Count	1 day
1.3.2	Message Supporters	1 day
1.3.3	Take Down Posters	5 days
1.3.4	Lessons Learned report	1 day
1.3.5	Project closure event	0 days

Quantifiable goals will help you measure the progress of your campaign. If by a certain date your team has knocked on 500 doors, is that good or bad? If your goal is 600, it is good; if your goal is 1,000, it is bad. If you have not set a quantifiable goal, you have no idea.

For each goal, plan the activities that will be required to reach that goal. If you plan to put up 200 posters by a certain date, by what date should you take your poster

19

design to the printer? When should you recruit the people necessary to put up 200 posters?

1.1.5.3   Resources

The roles and responsibilities are assigned to the various members of the project campaign team. The level of effort required by the resources named beside each activity indicates the % of their time each day. Where there is no % indicated, the resource is assigned 100% of their time for the duration of that activity. The material resources used for the completion of activities.

Legend for Resource Descriptions	
Resource	**Initials**
Candidate	C
Campaign Manager	CM
Finance Chair	FC
Press Secretary	PS
Office Manager	OM
Social Media Chair	SMC
Volunteers	Vol

1.1.5.3.1 Responsibility Assignments

Roles are defined by the tasks that need to be completed such that the campaign team members know their responsibilities. You might have people who fill more than one role. There are too many campaigns where someone is a volunteer, and they are unable to give a clear answer on what tasks they must accomplish. Many family members and friends may volunteer full time in a role out of loyalty to you as the candidate. These volunteers can be of great assistance accompanying you as the candidate, doing research on the opposition, helping with social media, brainstorming, or acting in a leader role for other volunteers. The more people you have actively involved in your campaign will result in less work for you and more time for you to concentrate on getting votes

WBS	Activity	Resources
1.1.1	The "As Is" Analysis	C
1.1.2	The "To Be" Analysis	CM [25%], C[25%]
1.1.3	Project Charter	C[25%], CM [25%],FC [25%], PS [25%], SMC[25%]
1.1.4.1.1	The Role of the Candidate	C
1.1.4.1.2	Select Campaign Manager	C[50%], CM [25%]
1.1.4.1.3	Select Campaign Team	C[50%], CM [50%]
1.1.4.2	Project Outputs	C[50%],FC [25%], CM [25%], OM [25%], PS [25%], SMC[25%]
1.1.4.3	Critical Success Factors	C[50%],FC [25%], CM [25%], OM [25%], PS [25%], SMC[25%]
1.1.4.4	Success Criteria	C[20%],FC [25%], CM [25%], OM [25%], PS [25%], SMC[25%]
1.1.4.5	Risk	C[50%],FC [25%], CM [25%], OM [25%], PS [25%], SMC[25%]

WBS	Activity	Resources
1.1.5.1	Work Breakdown Structure	C[50%],FC [25%], CM [25%], OM [25%], PS [25%], SMC[25%]
1.1.5.2	Time Schedule	C[50%],FC [25%], CM [25%], OM [25%], PS [25%], SMC[25%]
1.1.5.3.1	Responsibility Assignments	C[50%],FC [25%], CM [25%], OM [50%], PS [25%], SMC[25%]
1.1.5.3.2	Election Expenditure	C[50%],FC [25%], CM [25%], OM [50%], PS [25%], SMC[25%]
1.1.5.4.2	Resource Cost	C[50%],FC [50%]
1.2.1.1	Comply with Local Election Regulations	C[50%]
1.2.1.2	Register Candidacy	C[10%]
1.2.2.1	Define Campaign Structure	C[50%], CM [50%]
1.2.2.2	Organise Volunteers Roles	C[50%], CM [50%]

WBS	Activity	Resources
1.2.2.3	Upskill Volunteers	C[50%], CM [25%]
1.2.2.4	Seek Civic Groups Support	C[50%], CM [50%]
1.2.2.5	Political Party Support	C[50%], CM [50%]
1.2.2.6	Determine Volunteers Commitment	C[50%], CM [25%]
1.2.3.1	Do a SWOT Analysis of Yourself	C[10%]
1.2.3.2	Do a SWOT Analysis of Opponents	CM [10%], C[15%]
1.2.4.1	Examine the Electoral Register	C[10%], CM [10%]
1.2.4.2	Study Census Data	C[10%], CM [10%]
1.2.4.3	Look at the Geography of the Area	C[10%], CM [10%]

WBS	Activity	Resources
1.2.5.1	Geographic Targeting	C[10%], CM [10%]
1.2.5.2	Demographic Targeting	C[10%], CM [10%]
1.2.5.3	Non-Target Groups	C[10%], CM [5%]
1.2.5.4	Study Previous Election Statistics	C[20%], CM [10%]
1.2.6.1	Research Local Issues	C[10%], CM [10%], SMC[10%]
1.2.6.2	Message Style	C[10%], CM [10%], PS [10%], SMC[10%]
1.2.7.1	Door to Door Canvassing	C[35%], CM [25%],FC [25%], Vol1[25%], Vol2[25%], Vol3[25%],Vol 4[25%]
1.2.7.2	Literature Handouts	C[2%], CM [5%],FC [5%], Vol1[5%], Vol2[5%], Vol3[5%],Vol 4[5%]
1.2.7.3	Postal Mail	C[20%], OM [20%]
1.2.7.4	Get Out Your Vote	C[5%], CM [25%],FC [25%], Vol1[50%]

WBS	Activity	Resources
1.2.7.5	Posters	OM [20%], Vol1[50%]
1.2.7.6	Informal Meetings	C[5%], OM [20%]
1.2.7.7	Printed Press Media	C[10%], PS [50%]
1.2.7.8	Visual Media	C[10%], SMC[10%], OM [10%], PS [20%]
1.2.7.9	Website & Social Media	C[10%], SMC[20%], OM [20%], PS [20%]
1.2.7.10	Implement Polling Day Itinerary	C[50%]
1.3.1	The Count	C[20%], CM [20%], PS [20%], SMC[20%], OM [20%]
1.3.2	Message Supporters	C[10%], OM [10%], SMC[10%]
1.3.3	Take Down Posters	Vol1, Vol 2
1.3.4	Lessons Learned Report	C[50%], CM [50%]
1.3.5	Project Closure Event	C

1.1.5.3.2 Election Expenditure

Election spending incurred during the election campaign period must be disclosed by candidates and is subject to spending limits in some jurisdictions. For example, where spending limits apply posters or leaflets ordered and paid for before the election campaign, but used during the election spending period, must be accounted for.

Advertising: Expenses in respect of such advertising include agency fees, photography, design costs and other costs incurred in connection with preparing, producing, distributing, or otherwise disseminating such advertising on printed or on-line media. Schedule your orders so they are ready for the dates required and spread over the course of the campaign.

Election Posters: Place your order well in advance so that your posters are ready prior to the dates for erection. Expenses in respect of such material include the costs of the design, production, printing, erection, and removal of election posters. Expenses incurred in relation to paid election workers (for example, poster erectors) who are not in the employment of a political party, for refreshments and other minor out of pocket expenses are regarded as election expenses.

Other Election Material: Place your orders well in advance as suppliers will also be busy with orders for other candidates. Expenses in respect of such material include the design, production, printing, and dissemination of such material (other than posters), including canvas cards, election leaflets, election manifestos, newsletters, and other promotional election material.

Office and Stationery: Expenses in respect of those matters include costs incurred for office equipment, stationery, and postage.

Transport and Travel: Expenses incurred on transport and travel (by any means), petrol and diesel, rental or use of campaign vehicles, rental or use of vehicles for transport of voters on polling day, taxi and hackney services and courier services.

Campaign workers. Expenses include payments to campaign workers, insurance, and other costs.

1.1.5.4   Cost

Just about everything you do in the campaign will cost something either in hours or money. Estimate how much each of the tasks you hope to accomplish will cost and develop an overall budget for the entire campaign. Your campaign budget is a realistic list of what will be needed to implement your campaign plan. Written budgets are the only tools for tracking expenditures, providing goals, and keeping the candidate and campaign from spending without thinking.

Campaigns need to spend the bulk of their funds on voter contact activities. Administrative costs, including office machines, office staff, and phones, make up less than 20% of a campaign budget. Voter contact costs, including printed materials and door-to-door workers normally consume 70% to 80% of your financial resources.

The publication of material on the internet which is not related to the election period and predates this period does not need to be accounted for in the election expenses statement. This would include, for example, old press statements and publicity material that are still accessible on a website during the election spending period.

Certain features like populations served within the jurisdictions in which the elections take place may increase or decrease the expenditure levels. Those with large electorates may justify higher spending by candidates who cannot hope to exploit personal contact to the same degree they might in a less populated constituencies. Money matters in elections, and there is a positive link between expenditure and electoral success.

1.1.5.4.1 Spending and Donation Limits

Most countries have laws for controlling and limiting election expenditure by candidates. In such jurisdictions, parties and candidates must account for all that they spend on an election, including expenditure on advertising, promoting the party, opposing other candidates, and soliciting votes.

Some jurisdictions have also created a system of reimbursement of election expenses. If a candidate received at least a % of the quota of votes for the area in which he or she ran, he or she may apply for a reimbursement of up to a certain level of his or her election expenses.

Some countries have also introduced laws for controlling and limiting individual donation greater than a certain amount that candidates can receive for election expenses

In this context each candidate must familiarize themselves with the rules surrounding political donations, election expenses and reimbursements within the jurisdiction of the election.

Candidates may wish to appoint a Finance Chair to monitor and control the income and expenditure on the

elections as it may be an offence to spend over the limit, accept over-the-limit donations or fail to submit a statement of expenses to the relevant Public Office.

1.1.5.4.2 Resource Cost

The following represent potential cost items:

Item	Cost
Local Newspaper Ads	
Bulk Text Messaging	
Promotional Video	
Social Media Campaigns	
Election Posters	
Leaflets/Pamphlets	
Buttons	
Car Wrap	
Stickers	
Letter posted to households	
Personalised Pens	
Transport and Travel	
Campaign Workers	
Nomination/Registration Fee	

Determine an estimated cost by reviewing all your voter contact and other campaign activities. The rates and the estimated amount of time required from resources for this sample campaign are:

Resource Names	Units	Std. Rate
Candidate	411 hrs.	€/hr.
Campaign Manager	173 hrs.	€/hr.
Finance Chair	83 hrs.	€/hr.
Press Secretary	201 hrs.	€/hr.
Office Manager	166 hrs.	€/hr.
Social Media Chair	111 hrs.	€/hr.
Volunteer 1***	173 hrs.	€/hr.
Volunteer 2	48 hrs.	€/hr.
Volunteer 3	48 hrs.	€/hr.
Volunteer 4	48 hrs.	€/hr.

Note ***:

1. Most roles for local candidates are done free of charge by friends and relatives of the candidate. For this reason, we have only included the average time commitment for each role.
2. The number of volunteers required depends on the size of the constituency and the number of canvasses done in each area of the constituency.

1.2 Product Work Inputs

This section of the plan outlines the specifications for the election campaign to satisfy stakeholder requirements. The focus of the product work inputs is in attracting voters to your election platform and converting them to supporters. What you need to do here is determine what must be done to achieve that victory.

There are a lot of tasks that must be completed over the course of the campaign. A few of these tasks must wait

31

until the campaign is underway. Many of these tasks, such as all forms of voter persuasion, will be more effective if they are done closer to election day. However, voter persuasion and many other tasks can be made much easier if they are started well in advance of the actual campaign. Some of the tasks, such as examining past elections, can be completed before the campaign begins.

Potential candidates would benefit greatly if they would start viewing the political campaign as an ongoing process. The next campaign begins the day after the last election. Leaving all the work of campaigning until the election cycle begins makes all the work that much more difficult and decreases the chances that any of this work will be done well.

1.2.1   Election Requirements

Determine the type of election in which you will be running and what will be the rules of the election.

Announcement of Election

Following the announcement, that the election will be held on a given date, the campaign work commences in line with the product work inputs.

1.2.1.1   Comply with Local Election Regulations

Much of the basic strategy depends on this information. Missing a deadline or violating some part of the regulations could end your campaign before it has even begun. These rules are the constitution for participants in elections. Adherence to these rules is key and in-depth

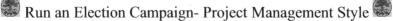

knowledge of the monitoring processes is a must to ensure your competitors are also adhering to the rules.

Eligibility

To run as a candidate for election in most countries you must be:

• A citizen of that country

• Over 18 years of age and in some countries, this can be 21 or over.

• Register as a candidate by a certain date and pay a registration fee.

Disqualified Persons

Depending on the country certain people are disqualified from becoming members of their jurisdiction's parliament:

• An elected member of another Office, Parliament, Court or Whole Time Civil Servants are prohibited from holding elected membership of a public office and such another occupation at the same time.

• People currently imprisoned and persons of unsound mind.

• People who have been convicted of fraud or dishonest dealings, corrupt practice or acting while disqualified.

1.2.1.2   Register Candidacy

If you wish to be nominated to stand for election to parliament in your jurisdiction, there is usually a specific time frame in which you must be nominated. You must complete and submit your nomination paper to the appropriate office for your constituency in which you are standing for election by a certain date.

1.2.2   Organise Campaign Team

In order to accomplish activities such as press conferences, putting up and taking down posters, handling queries, dealing with printers, distributing literature and engaging with voters etc., you will need a well organised and structured campaign team.

1.2.2.1   Define Campaign Structure

Determine and outline the campaign team member roles and accountability for tasks and communicate these and the support mechanisms to everyone involved in the campaign.

1.2.2.2   Organise Volunteers Roles

If you are going to accomplish everything necessary, you will need a lot of help and you probably will not be able to pay them. This is where volunteer support comes in. People volunteer for many reasons and can come from many different areas. The first volunteers are mostly friends and relatives of the candidate and party activists (if you are a party candidate) who have worked on past campaigns. Look for people who have volunteered in other areas of their life. They may volunteer for civic organisations, resident's association, schools, or sports clubs. If your campaign message speaks to a particular issue or group, you may be able to persuade an organisation involved in that issue to support you and provide volunteers. As your campaign talks to voters you should take every opportunity to ask people to help the campaign. If you are attached to a party, party loyalists become involved out of a sense of commitment to the party. Some people volunteer because they feel strongly about a particular issue and either believes you agree with them on that issue or your opponent is bad on that issue. Some people are just social and become involved with the political campaign because of friends or others who share their interests.

Volunteers stay with a campaign because they feel that they are contributing, because they feel appreciated, because the work is interesting, because they are meeting interesting people, and because it is fun. Volunteers can burn out if they are giving too much work but more likely they will leave the campaign because they became bored or feel that the work they are given does not matter.

Determine how many volunteers you will need at which times to complete the objectives you have set for yourself. Again, you will be able to work this out from the project schedule. For example, suppose you decide you want to canvass 1,000 households in a particular neighborhood on a particular Saturday morning. You decide that one volunteer can canvass an average of 50 households in 3 hours. Therefore, it will take 20 volunteer's hours to accomplish the job in three hours. You will also need to have the literature ready by Saturday, you will need to have some maps of the area and clear instructions for the volunteers and you will need to have someone responsible for overseeing the canvass drop and knows what is supposed to happen. You may also have to provide transportation to the target neighborhood. Volunteers are just that, volunteers. You need to do this type of calculation for every part of your voter contact plan and the more detail you can provide the better. Therefore, planning is critical. There is often one person, a volunteer coordinator, who is responsible for training volunteers, making sure they have the materials they need and making sure everything goes as planned.

1.2.2.3   Upskill Volunteers

Once your campaign determines what message will persuade your target voters to vote for you, then you must get your volunteers repeat that same message at every opportunity. Just because you say something does not mean they are listening or will remember what you said. For your message to register with the voters, they must hear the same message many times in many ways.

Train your volunteers to find out which candidate voters support just by asking them and record their answer. Equip each volunteer with the details of each household from the register of electors. Getting contact details mobile number, email address for your supporters at this stage would be of enormous benefit when trying to get people out to vote. People generally like to be asked their opinion and are willing to tell you what they are thinking. Develop a simple "1-2-3" scale for your volunteers so that a confirmed supporter is labeled a "1," an undecided voter is a "2," and a supporter of an opponent is a "3." As your campaign communicates with voters, try to judge their level of support. You will want to spend most of your resources on number "2" voters in your target audience. Because so much of the Get Out To Vote (GOTV) effort relies on having an accurate list of supporters well in advance of Election Day, it is important to know how you will identify supporters starting early in the campaign. You need to spend resources persuading your voters. However, if you only communicate with them, you are relying on them to go to the polls on polling day. You can increase your chances if you know who has been convinced and you can get them to the polls.

Train volunteers to accomplish three things to varying degrees during door to door canvassing - persuade target voters, identify voters as supporters, undecided or otherwise, and turnout your vote as No. 1 or 2 preference.

1.2.2.4   Seek Civic Groups Support

Civic organisations can play an important role in your election campaign. Make a list of all the civic groups and other organisations that are likely to be supportive of your campaign, in the early stages of the campaign. List the contact person with each organisation, the phone number and any other information that would be helpful in contacting the group.

Determine how these groups could best be of assistance to your campaign. Bear in mind that coalition and collaboration is a two-way street. What will support groups expect from you in return for their assistance and what are you prepared to deliver?

1.2.2.5   Political Party Support

If you are running as a party candidate, your political party should have an overall message of why voters should support you as its candidate. Assuming you agree with this message and your individual message corresponds to this national message, the party may be able to provide you with general material. Your national party may provide information about policy initiatives at the national level.

National political parties can help you design your campaign materials to match the national message. The party may have contract negotiated with printers and other vendors to produce all or much of the materials, thus gaining a saving in price for all its candidates. The national party may be able to provide posters, leaflets, or calendars that you give to supporters.

The visit of the national party leader can often draw local attention to your campaign and photos of you as the candidate with the national party leader can be used in campaign materials.

1.2.2.6 Determine Volunteer Commitment

Based on all the activities your campaign intends to accomplish, determine how many volunteers you will need to reasonably accomplish each activity you have listed in your campaign project schedule. You can then estimate how many volunteers you will need throughout the campaign. Be as specific as possible, using real numbers. How much of a task can one volunteer accomplish in one hour and how many volunteer hours will it take to accomplish the whole activity? How many pieces of literature do you need to deliver? How many homes do you want to visit in how much time?

1.2.3 Research Candidates

Compare and contrast the demographic profiles (age, gender, profession, education, etc.) of all the candidates, including yourself. Compare and contrast the campaign messages of your opponents to those of your own.

1.2.3.1   Conduct a SWOT Analysis of Yourself

Determine your true strengths and weaknesses from your friends, family, and colleagues. The most important factor in your election will be you as the candidate. As you do this exercise, look at yourself from the point of view of your opponent. What you may view as a new approach, your opponent may view old hack.

You may want to sort your SWOT assessment into various sections, such as childhood, education, work history, immediate family, and past political positions.

By finding your weaknesses early, the campaign will be better prepared to deal with them and respond to charges that may come up later in the campaign. Too many candidates have lost because they refused to deal with past mistakes and were caught off guard when their opponents painted the picture of their mistakes in a very unflattering light.

1.2.3.2   Conduct a SWOT Analysis of Opponents

Once you have determined your own strengths and weaknesses, the next logical step is to repeat the process for your opponents'. If there are several opponents, determine your strongest competitors for the loyalty of voters you hope to attract. Organise your assessment into various sections and look for both strengths weaknesses opportunities and threats.

Your opponents will not be forthcoming with information about themselves. You will probably need to do some digging to find reasons for voters to vote against them and for you.

Look for patterns of behavior and past policies that you can use to persuade voters to either vote against your opponent or for you. You can use this research to create a contrast between your campaign and your opponents' campaign and be prepared for what your opponent will say and do. Be meticulous and well organised as you gather your opposition research. Double check and list the sources of your documentation. Be able to back-up your information with factual data.

1.2.4 Examine Demographics

Use the electoral register and Census data to break the voters in your electoral area into manageable groups to develop a strategy for targeting voters and determining what you need to accomplish to win. Use the electoral area dimensions to calculate the number of posters you must put up.

1.2.4.1 Examine the Electoral Register

The Electoral Register is the go-to file for an accurate list of all possible voters available to the campaign and eligible vote in this election. Use the register to identify potential supporters who are not on the register and encourage them to register in time to cast their vote. Use the number of voters, houses, and apartments to calculate the number of brochures you need to distribute and the number of doors you must knock on.

You can reduce this group yet again. On average, let us say that there are two voters per household. Some families may have three or four voters living in the same house. Some voters may be single and live alone. The bottom line is to determine how many households you need to communicate with to receive the number of votes needed to win?

1.2.4.2   Study Census Data

"Total population" is all the people who live in your district. Considering children too young to vote and people not registered in the district, this number should be larger than the total number of voters. Use the Electoral Register in association with census data and any other local databases to determine:

1. The support available for various political parties.
2. The demographic composition of the voters as defined by characteristics such as age, sex, and marital status. Voters with similar characteristics may have similar interests and may tend to vote the same way. Seniors will be less interested in schools and more interested in pensions while young mothers will be more interested in schools and less interested in pensions. By determining how many senior citizens there are and how many young mothers there are, you will be better able to target your message to groups that matter to your success.
3. The income levels, education levels and professions of the voters.
4. The geographic break down of the voters in terms of percentage or how many people live in the city, in the rural areas or in small villages.
5. The type of accommodation the voters live in.

1.2.4.3 Look at the Geography of the Area

Gather information on the district such as:

1. The area of the district in which you will be running.
2. The type of terrain will you have to cover as you campaign.
3. The type of transportation you need to use.

Use maps to plan your routes and identify meeting points.

1.2.5 Target Voters

Too often campaigns forget to calculate how many votes will be needed to guarantee victory and determining where these votes will come from. They then spend their precious resources of time, money and people trying to talk to the whole population instead of the much fewer voters they will need to win. Here you will reduce the number of voters with whom you need to communicate to a much more manageable size. As part of your research to now, you have determine the total population of your district, the total number of voters, the expected votes cast, the number of votes needed to win and the number of households in which these voters live. Some of the answers that are needed here require you to investigate the future and make some educated guesses. Use your best judgment and the information you have found from past elections. The point of targeting is to determine which subsets of the voting population are most likely to be responsive to you as the candidate and focusing your campaign efforts on these groups of voters.

There are three types of voters: your supporters, your opponents' supporters and those voters in the middle who have yet to make up their minds. Your supporters are those who have already decided to vote for you. Your opponents' supporters are those who have already decided to vote for your opponents. Those voters in the middle who have not yet decided and still need to be persuaded to vote for one or the other candidates are called "undecided" voters. It is some portion of these "undecided" voters whom you want to target and with whom you want to communicate your message. If you fail in getting a no. 1 vote, ask for a 2nd preference vote in a ranked voting system. The following chart provides one model of how to relate targeting to your campaign efforts:

Effort	Category	Groups
33%	People who are most likely to vote you No. 1	
33%	Potential supporters who may be persuaded to vote you No. 1	
15%	People who are most likely to vote you No. 2	
15%	Potential voters who may be persuaded to vote you No. 2	
4%	People who are not likely to support you	

1.2.5.1   Geographic Targeting

Geographic targeting is simply determining who will vote for you based on where they live. It is generally accepted that undecided voters are most likely to be persuaded by a campaign's efforts. Because of this, most campaigns spend most of their effort - posters, door to door, etc. - in areas with high rates of undecided voters.

Your campaign plan may include different tactics for different areas. For example, the plan may call for a lot of posters and volunteer calling in areas expected to be supportive. On the other hand, you as the candidate may want to personally go door to door in areas with a high level of undecided voters. However while an area may have a very high level of undecided voters," past turnout may indicates that few people living in that area will actually vote and you as the candidate should not waste your time with inactive voters.

Answer the following questions to determine the geographic targeting for your campaign:

1. Where do all the candidates live? Are there any distinct geographic areas of support for any candidate? A 2nd preference vote in a geographical area where support is high for a weaker candidate can help you get over the line if that candidate is eliminated early in mixed voting or ranked system where votes are transferred.

2. What are the past performances of candidates in each district of the electoral area?

3. What is the expected turnout of each district of the electoral area?

1.2.5.2   Demographic Targeting

Demographic targeting is not an exact science and can be made more difficult by the lack of available, accurate demographic data. Nevertheless, it is important to do this exercise and look to target 1st and 2nd preferences. Many candidates in the past have lost largely due to a failure to define a target audience for 1st preferences and a target audience for 2nd preferences that are likely to transfer. Candidates, when asked to identify their audience tended to respond by naming every demographic subset. In this instance, they had no target audience because their target audience was everybody.

When determining which groups can be persuaded to vote for a candidate, look for groups to which you as the candidate belong. Say you as the candidate are a 40-year-old, college educated small businessman, married with a son and a daughter in school, living in a city suburb in the area. Your target groups are going to be young people between the ages of 25 and 40, small businesspeople, and parents with school age children. You are less likely to appeal to groups of the voting population to which you do not belong. You will have less appeal to pensioners, workers with less education, and farmers from the rural part of the district. If there are enough votes in your target groups to win and you are the best candidate to appeal to these voters, then you need only to communicate a persuadable message to this group throughout the campaign to win.

There are two things that can make this targeting less likely to work. First, the demographic groups you choose are too small. Second, there are other candidates with similar backgrounds who are appealing to the same group. In both cases, if another candidate is also appealing to this same group or it is not a large enough part of the population to provide the margin of victory, then the campaign needs to look to collateral groups or those groups nearest in interests for further support. In the above example you may want to expand your message to include more people. You will not win 100% of the vote of any population but if you can expect to receive 4or 5 out of every 10 votes, then this is a group of voters with whom you should be in touch.

1.2.5.3   Non-Target Groups

An important part of demographic targeting is determining which demographic groups will not be part of your targeted audience. During your strategic planning session, you should, for example, state explicitly "we will not target certain workers or certain age groups. This exercise will help you avoid the trap of defining too wide a targeted audience. This type of non-targeting applies to social media campaigns, leaflet distribution and your campaign message and not to door to door canvassing.

1.2.5.4   Study Previous Election Statistics

Get valuable information about this election by looking at information from past elections. Study the candidates who ran for election in your area in past elections and the results. Evaluate the voter's turnout out for similar elections in the past and the number of votes that were needed to get elected. Use this type of information to predict the turnout and baseline levels of support in this election.

"Expected turnout" is the expected number of votes to be cast in this election. Not every voter will vote and all other things being equal you can estimate how many voters will vote by looking at past similar elections. If there was 35% turn out in the last similar election and there are no added factors to change the situation, you might figure that about 35% would vote in the election this time.

1.2.6   Develop Campaign Message

You have now determined who the best audience for your message will be. This is the foundation to help you determine what you can say that is likely to persuade them to vote for you. An important rule to remember about a campaign message is that as a candidate tries to reach a broader and broader audience, then that candidate's message becomes defused and weaker for each part of that audience. Ultimately, the party or candidate that promises everything to everybody has an empty message that no voter will find credible or compelling.

Your campaign message tells the voters why you are running for this office and why they should choose you over your opponents for the same office. Be mindful that you and your election campaign are low in the average voter's list of priorities and that voters are being bombarded with information every day.

A campaign message is not simply the candidate's program of what they will do if elected, or a list of the issues the candidate will address, and it is not a simple, catchy phrase or slogan. All of these things can be part of a campaign message, depending on whether or not they will persuade voters, but they should not be confused with the message, a simple statement that will be repeated over and over throughout the campaign to persuade your target voters. Once you have developed a clear, concise, persuadable message it is important that you use that message at every opportunity and not deviate from it throughout the campaign.

That is why they come up with a clear, concise message and spend a lot of money making sure their target audience sees and hears that message as many times as possible.

1.2.6.1   Research the Local Issues

As stated above, your campaign message is not your program or the list of issues you will address. Still, your campaign should address the issues that are important to your target voters.

Example 1

Do you want a fresh approach to [the provision of housing], or continuation of what we have?

Do you want a fresh approach to [public expenditure], or continuation of what we have?

Example 2

[Candidate] stands for action on [issue 1], one step at the time.

[Candidate] stands for action on [issue 2], one step at the time.

It is important not to confuse a problem with an issue. A problem is a condition that needs addressing, such as economic problems. An issue is a solution or partial solution to a problem, such as increased investment in education and small business to address problems with the economy.

As you consider what issues your campaign will address through its message, there are two important things to remember. First, how important is this issue to your target voters? Second, which candidate has the better position on this issue in the eyes of the voters? Too often, candidates either focus on issues that are not important to voters, ignoring more important issues, or they focus on issues where their opponents' can claim with a certain amount of credibility or a better position on the issue.

Having determined a target audience for your campaign, the next step is to get to understand the members of this target audience thoroughly in terms of their issues.

Research in detail the issues that will make voters take notice during this election. In general, be familiar with and prioritise the areas your target voters are more concerned about:

Economic Issues: - Government Investment for Job creation etc.
Social Issues: - Acquisition of land banks to address Housing Shortage, etc.
External Issues: - International Rapid Response to Curb Pandemics, etc.

Suppose you are considering ten issues that may become factors in the upcoming election campaign. You want to concentrate on only two or three. Rank 5 - 10 issues (1 through 10) in order of importance to your target voters

1.2.6.2   Message Style

There are several criteria that make up a strong message.
1. Keep it short and be able to deliver it to a voter in less than one minute.
2. Deliver your message in a clear unambiguous language that voters understand easily.
3. Create a visual image of your message in the minds of voters by portraying real life situations.
4. In campaign literature use photos showing you as the candidate talking to someone or doing

something. For example, a picture of rubbish dumped illegally on the cover of piece of literature dealing with crime will mean that voters are more likely to open it to see what it is about. The inside photo could show you as the candidate talking to the police, thereby making the connection between the issue and the candidate. Too often literature only has a portrait photo of the candidate. This does not tell the voter anything about the candidate.

5. Write the headline as a brief statement or summary of the whole message.

6. Use, bullet points in the text rather than put it in paragraph form.

7. Be as specific as possible in offering solutions to the problems people face. The candidate "supports legislation that will..." does not mean that the legislation must pass or accomplish the goal, but it still conveys a stand on an issue. It is important to back up your statements about understanding a problem or issue with evidence of experience or knowledge from your personal past.

Base your campaign's message on solid research. Use some research method like focus groups made up of representatives of local organisations to test your campaign's message before the start of the election campaign. Why publicise a message without testing it to see whether it will be effective?

Now that you have a clear, concise, and effective message, it is important to use that message to persuade your target group of voters that you are the best choice. Voters need to know what your message is, and they need to hear it many times for it to register with them. There is no point in having a great message if the voters do not know about it.

1.2.7   Implement Voter Contact Plan

Dependent on your level of finite resources in terms of time, money, and people there are various methods of getting your campaign's message out to voters. The objective is to select the best possible combination and use all three resources in the most efficient manner. You want to make the largest impact on the voters for each volunteer hour and each amount of money you spend.

You need to first figure out what you want to accomplish and then figure out which of the many ways is best for you achieve your objective. If one method does not seem possible, you can often find another method. Therefore, planning is necessary. It is the campaign that does not have a written plan which often finds that it does not have the money it needs; does not have the volunteers it needs and has squandered its time.

Make a list of all the methods you have decided to use in your campaign and try to determine in hard numbers how much time, money, and people you will need to accomplish your objective.

You also must understand how voters get their information. What are the local media outlets? Who are the reporters and what are their deadlines? How will the election be covered and how does the press view the various candidates? To develop a comprehensive press strategy, it is important to have as much information on the media as possible.

1.2.7.1 Door to Door Canvassing

One of the most effective ways to persuade voters is for volunteers to go from house to house, apartment to apartment, door-to-door talking to individual voters one at a time leaving a piece of literature about you as the candidate at each household. Many volunteers can cover a large area relatively quickly and, because you know that the houses are in the voting district, you know that only potential voters are being reached. The volunteers talk with voters, so they identify supporters, and they can leave literature with a note for those voters not at home when they called.

Break the electoral area up into sections and assign teams of trained volunteers to cover each area. In so doing you can hear the problems voters face, tailor your message to meet their individual concerns and ascertain your level of support. Often voters are impressed that a candidate would bother to come meet them and you can gain their support just by making the effort.

This is a time-consuming method of voter contact. Depending on the types of neighborhoods you will be walking in, a candidate who is disciplined can talk to approximately 50 voters a night or around 300 voters a week. This is assuming that you canvas for about three hours a night and spend no more than three minutes with each voter (allowing a little bit of time to get from door to door). Now you understand why you must be able to deliver your message in less than a minute.

Because door to door is so time consuming, there are several things you can do to make it more effective and make sure you stay on schedule. Once again, these things require forethought and planning. You may consider adapting these methods to fit your circumstances.

Voters are more likely to remember a candidate's message if they hear it more than once, so a candidate is more likely to make an impression if they can increase their voter contact at the door from one time to two, three or four times. Generally, candidates aim to cover their electoral area twice and visiting each household once. This can be done by first having the campaign deliver a piece of literature to homes, introducing the candidate and asking about local issues and documenting support levels. This can be either mailed to isolated districts or dropped by volunteers and should deliver the campaign message.

Starting early and being organised are probably the most important ingredients in winning an election. To win, you have one simple goal - to get more votes than your competition. The earlier you start, the more time you will have to get more votes. The second canvass will take place close to polling day. The candidate walks the neighborhoods delivering the message both verbally and through a piece of literature that is left with the voter. This time the candidate will ask for a vote, a no 1, 2 or 3.

A well organised campaign is able to keep track of who the candidate talked to and who was missed, it will be able to deliver a follow-up message later, stating that the candidate was either happy to have met the voter or sorry to have missed them.

The best way to keep the canvass on schedule is to have a trusted volunteer accompany you as the candidate as they go door to door. This person is responsible for carrying all the literature, knocking on the doors, and introducing you as the candidate when someone answers the door. The volunteer keeps a record of which doors are answered and which not.

As the election period draws to a close, there comes a time when you can no longer persuade voters and your efforts should be spent on making sure that those people who support you, turnout to vote for you.

To do this, you must have some way of identifying who supports you and who has been persuaded through your voter contact effort to support you. Well before election day you must have spent time identifying your supporters. It is also important to know how you will reach them in a noticeably short period of time.

As you identify voters as outlined in upskilling volunteers, you will want to have some method of keeping track of them and their levels of support. You can use a simple database that you can continuously update and sort to meet your needs. It is important that this database be as accurate as possible. Do not consider someone a supporter unless they have told you so directly.

The number one factor in helping people decide to whom they will give their vote is not policy, or party affiliation. It is whether they have met the candidate in person.

1.2.7.2   Literature Handouts

Your campaign can also hand out literature wherever people gather in large numbers. This could be at markets, factory gates, bus/train stations, shopping centres, etc. While this may be a lot easier or quicker than the literature drop at the voters' homes, it is less targeted because you are not certain that the people who take your literature live in the district or can vote for you.

Often this type of activity is targeted around a particular issue that will concern those gathered in that area. For example, you may want to hand out a piece of literature about saving hospital services at the gates of the hospital.

1.2.7.3 Postal Mail

Sending campaign literature to voters in isolated areas through the mail can be highly effective at delivering your message and persuading them to vote for you. Depending on what type of list you have, you may be able to target voters either by geography or demographics (age, gender, etc.). For example, you could send something outlining your stand on one issue to senior citizens and send a different piece outlining your stand on a different issue to young women. Again, you will know that those who receive your mail live in the district.

Posting campaign literature to voters in local elections is an expensive method of communicating compared to SMS text messaging and social media messaging. This method can only be considered for voters living in remote areas unless a subsidy exists.

1.2.7.4 Get Out Your Vote

It does no good to have spent months persuading your target audience that you are the best candidate if they do not go to the polls on election day and vote for you. Individual voters often feel that their one single vote does not matter. They need to know that they are part of something bigger and that their support for you is important. Often a simple reminder –a phone call, a social media message, a text or piece of literature - can be enough to ensure that they vote.

The deadline for all the campaign and particularly the get out the vote (GOTV) part of the campaign is the close of the polls on election day. Either you are prepared to make that final push, or you are not. There are no second chances.

Once you have developed a database or list of supporters, it is important to have the resources and the means of communicating with them in the short period of time just before the election. It is therefore important to budget enough time, money and people and have a realistic plan of how you will get in touch with your supporters.

1.2.7.5 Posters

Visibility is anything the campaign does to catch the voters' eye. This can be signs by the side of the road (with planning permission if needed), signs at supporters houses, posters on poles, stickers on cars, decorated cars driving through key neighborhoods, your (the candidate) name on tee-shirts, coffee mugs, etc. While this may raise the voter awareness about the campaign and the name recognition of your candidacy, it can only reinforce the campaign message. It is an extremely poor method of persuading voters. It also reaches a broad audience rather than a targeted audience. People who live outside the district or otherwise cannot or will not vote for you will see the signs. Finally, there is no way of identifying who is supporting your candidacy. However, this method can be used very effectively to remind voters in strong support areas to go vote.

Be aware of litter pollution when displaying election posters and be aware of any regulations stating that posters must be removed within a certain period after polling day by the candidate or party. It is good practice to check out posters erected on poles to ensure they are pointing in the right direction and are not causing a hazard to motorists or pedestrians. Sometimes they can be blown inwards with wind gusts and become invisible to traffic.

1.2.7.6   Informal Meetings

Ask friends and supporters if they could invite friends to meet you as the candidate in their homes. These have the advantage of face-to-face contact with you as the candidate and can also be used for volunteer recruitment. Although a good coffee morning or tea party program can be difficult to organise, the campaign should consider organising at least one or two per targeted area.

1.2.7.7   Printed Press Media

Elections are such rare events that they receive considerably more press than many other events in the same area. The press is a source of information outside the campaign, and voters often respect it. Use newspapers, to get your campaign message out. It helps to have a press secretary with established good relationships with print and broadcast journalists in your region. The printed media is free of cost and every time a journalist prints or broadcasts a story about your campaign, you have the opportunity to get your message out to your target audience at no direct money cost to your campaign.

Voters are much more likely to believe positive information about your campaign if it comes from an "independent" printed source. If you have a press secretary, it is their responsibility for maintaining a good relationship with the press and communicating with the press. The press secretary is expected to have a list of all the media outlets in the area, complete with reporters' names, phone numbers and deadlines.

It is important that you make the job of writing about the campaign as easy as possible for the reporters. At the same time, make sure that everything is clear and reinforces your message. Press conferences should be well scripted and be important enough that it is worth the time of the press to come to them.

1.2.7.8   Audio/Visual Media

Unfortunately, you will not be able to count on journalists to provide you with all the publicity you will need for your campaign. You may need to purchase additional publicity in the forms of newspaper radio or television advertisements.

Local Radio stations often offer election candidates an opportunity to get their election manifestos and messages aired. Listeners may be given the opportunity to quiz candidates on issues. Such opportunities are invaluable so you need to know exactly what you will say and practice saying it and within a given time limit if stipulated. Be well prepared for the difficult questions that may be fired at you while on air.

Paying for TV advertisements is rare in localised elections and candidates must examine the return on investment for such an outlay. Localised campaigns for candidates not belonging to a Party may not be able to afford the amount of money television would cost to reach a small number of voters.

This is a less targeted way to reach voters than canvassing the district or sending direct mail because, while you reach a broad audience, again it is not clear that everyone who hears or sees your advertisement is able to vote for you or is in your target audience. Still, this can be a very persuasive form of communication with voters, particularly television. It is particularly good at reinforcing a message that is delivered in person, such as door to door.

If you get the opportunity to do a TV broadcast or appearance undergo some form of media training or preparation in advance as television appearances are rare and precious. Before any television appearance, know exactly what you will say and practice saying it.

1.2.7.9   Website & Social Media

Website:

If you do not have one, create and place a web page on the Internet. You may be able to get some press from introducing your web site and while it can be an inexpensive way to convey a lot of information to those who are interested, it can be used as an effective way at reaching a particular, targeted audience.

Social Media:

Understand the power of social media for their campaigns and which channels you should use. When sharing the same content on more than one platform leave a couple of hours between the times when you are online and posting the same content on different platforms.

With the varying resources of time, money and people, the combination of voter contact methods that can be combined is unlimited and no two campaigns will ever be alike. Therefore, it is vitally important to take all the data possible on the district, the voters, and all the candidates, and then the campaign must develop a workable, written plan to deliver the message. Videos and pictures of the campaign in progress can be made into content for posting on social media.

People are often persuaded when they hear the same thing from many different sources. If they hear that you are a good candidate from a well-known civic organisation, meet you going door to door, see some campaign literature, and read an article about you in the newspaper, than they will more likely remember you and more likely vote for you as that candidate. None of these contacts should be left to chance.

A well organised campaign will make sure that all these contacts happen and that the same message is delivered each time so that the message reinforces itself each time.

Email:

The ability to send emails to supporters and voters can be a power tool for your campaign but if you are not careful with GDPR, you can get hurt.

1.2.7.10 Implement Polling Day Itinerary

Set out an hour by hour timetable for the day of the election and adhere to the activities. It is easy to take your eye off the ball as the campaign ends. An itinerary will help to keep all the team focused. Send out timed Emails, Texts, Facebook, and Twitter reminders, to drive voters to the polls and help them find their voting locations.

Keep in mind that the team needs to be provided with refreshments throughout the day. Make sure someone oversees keeping canvassers and other volunteers fed and happy. Consider midday lunch with team and volunteers to update them on the day's progress and energise them again later with food for the afternoon and evening push.

1.3 Closeout

Project Closeout sees the formal end of the project. The closeout will verify that the objectives have been accomplished.

1.3.1   The Count

Invite your team to the count centre. Arrange for refreshments for your team during the count. Congratulate any candidates that become elected and commiserate with all candidates who are eliminated.

1.3.2   Message Supporters

Advise all your supporters of your result and thank them for their support. This can be done by phone text or social media. Repeat the exercise in the same fashion as you did for the GOTV message.

1.3.3   Take Down Posters

Take down all posters and campaign signs. Place re-usable poster material in a suitable location.

1.3.4   Lessons Learned report

The identification and recording of issues arising on the project will help to reduce or eliminate the chances of re-occurrence on similar projects in the future. A "lessons learned" report is completed immediately after Election Day and details incorporated into future project plans.

1.3.5   **Project closure event**

To signal the end of the project, hold an informal gathering
to recognise the work completed by the team.

Printed in Great Britain
by Amazon

53890181R00038